THINK DIFFERENTLY

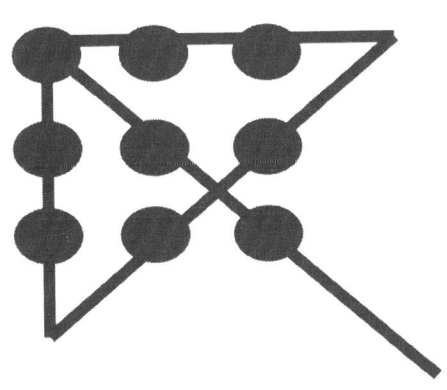

To Achieve Amazing Success

2nd Edition
Dr. Kevin C. Snyder

Copyright 2012 © by Kevin C. Snyder

All rights reserved. No part of this publication may be reproduced, stored in a retrieval system, or in any form by any means, except in brief quotations in a review, without the express written consent of the individual author.

All quotes contained within this book are written by the author unless credit is specifically given to another source.

ISBN-13: 978-1478247210
ISBN-10: 1478247215

Bulk rate discounted purchasing is available though contacting the publishing coordinator listed below or by contacting one of the authors.

2nd Edition Edited by Inspir-Active Solutions
Layout and Design by Inspir-Active Solutions
Cover Design by Matthew Bonazzoli (www.dvdocument.com)

For Additional Information:
Dr. Kevin C. Snyder
www.kevincsnyder.com
www.InspirActiveSolutions.com

About The Author

Kevin Snyder has helped thousands of leaders take action and lead more fulfilling and passionate lives. As both a professional speaker, inventor, author, and student affairs professional, Kevin knows what styles of leadership programs captivate, inspire, and entertain audiences.

Kevin has held professional positions as an educational consultant, trainer, and higher education administrator in areas of Student Activities, Greek Life, Orientation Services, Counseling, Academic Advising and Residence Life. Most recently, he served as Dean of Students for High Point University in High Point, North Carolina. He is also an adjunct faculty member at the Center for Creative Leadership based in Greensboro, North Carolina.

Kevin is a professional facilitator and speaker with years of experience presenting keynotes, retreats, and values-based leadership programs. Kevin's keynotes and workshops have given him the privilege of speaking in front of audiences across the country. Over 300 audiences in all 50 states have experienced his energetic, inspirational, and motivating programs.

He received his undergraduate degree in marine biology from the University of North Carolina at Wilmington where he was awarded both *Homecoming King* and *Greek Man of the Year*! His master's degree is from the University of South Carolina where he was also awarded Graduate Student of the Year. His doctorate in Educational Leadership was earned from the University of Central Florida. Kevin is a member and former traveling consultant for Delta Tau Delta Fraternity and staff member aboard Semester at Sea.

Speaking Topics

Dr. Snyder has presented to over 300 college campuses, conferences, corporations, churches, and civic groups on the following topics:

~ Motivation & leadership
~ Goal setting & team building
~ Personal and professional growth
~ Effective communication
~ Eating disorders and wellness

Book Kevin for
~ Upbeat, motivational conference keynotes
~ Campus-wide leadership programs and retreats
~ Corporate and civic meetings and retreats
~ Greek Life events such as banquets, seminars, new member programs and *Greek Week*
~ Orientation and New Student seminars and activities
~ Housing and Residence Life programs

For speaking information and availability, contact:

www.kevincsnyder.com or www.InspirActiveSolutions.com

"It's impossible to lose if you never give up."

Dedicated to **You**.

Identify and pursue your passions with conviction.

Live a fulfilled life.

To Your Success,

Kevin

"Life has a tendency to live up to the expectations we have for it."

Table of Contents

Think Differently 10

I Lived My Dream 27

Passion 36

Lessons of Wisdom 44

Your Greatest Accomplishment 54

The Power of Choice 61

The Secret 75

More to The Secret 82

Mastering the Art of Effective Communication 94

Gratitude 100

The Essence of Survival 102

A Wish For Leaders 104

Motivation Matters! 105

For more information 113

Think Differently

"You become _____ the moment you decide to be."
(fill in the blank)

<u>Thinking differently</u> – the fundamental concept within this book. Thinking differently is also an essential concept for living a successful, and more importantly, a fulfilling life.

Each of us has absolute control over but one thing, and that is our thoughts! The way we think determines how we feel, and how we feel dictates how we act. Our thoughts manifest an outcome, and our actions and behaviors can be changed at any moment simply by recognizing the power of our thoughts. No matter where you've been and where you are in life, today depends on you. Today depends on the choices you make right now.

THE PAST DOES <u>NOT</u> EQUAL THE FUTURE!

Today is the most important day of your life simply because you are exchanging a day of your own life for it. Why not choose to live it accordingly, with passion and purpose. Why not choose to make a difference? Why not choose to think differently?

We all have a story – this book is mine. Each chapter is a different lesson I've learned and I thank God that I have been able to learn from my mistakes and become a better person as a result. Mistakes are lessons of wisdom, when you ask yourself the right questions. And when you lose, don't lose the lesson.

11

Look at the nine dots below.

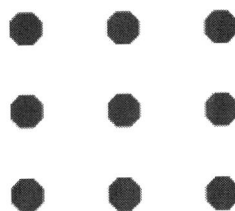

Now with your finger or a pencil, try to connect all nine dots with four straight, connected lines. Meaning, each of the four straight lines is connected to the next.

Go ahead, complete this activity. Do not continue until you've spent at least one minute trying to connect all nine dots!

Were you successful at connecting all nine dots with four straight lines?

If so, congratulations, *but* you probably have seen this exercise before! If not, you are not alone. I typically use this activity in my motivational presentations for college campuses and businesses. To date, I have spoken in front of more than 100,000 people, and not one person has ever successfully completed this exercise who did not know how to do it beforehand.

On the next page is the strategy you would use to accomplish the task:

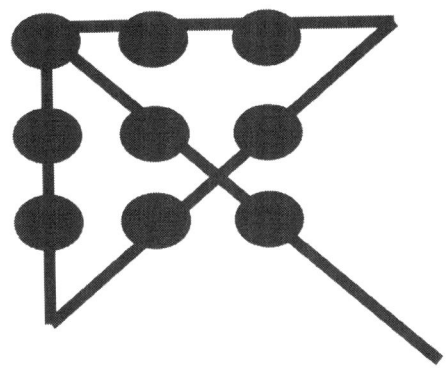

As you can see, in order to achieve the task you must think "outside the box." Most likely, you have heard this expression before, but most of us, unfortunately, do *not* understand how important this concept is in life.

In order to achieve what we truly want and desire, we must *think differently*, outside the box. Only then, will we experience life and accomplish the dreams and goals we aspire to and have the full potential for.

This area within the box is where we feel safe. It is an internal feeling which we associate as a "comfort zone."

We all have a comfort zone and each one is different. Some are naturally larger and some are smaller than others. But it is when we stay within this comfort zone that we prevent ourselves from achieving the goals we desire and are capable of.

> *The only limitations we have are the ones*
> *we mentally place there.*
> ~ Franklin Roosevelt, Former U.S. President

We all like to stay within our comfort zone, because, understandably it is where we feel safe. It is where we feel in control and most likely where we've been before. But again, the paradigm you must understand is that our comfort zones also place limitations on us. By not going outside our comfort zones, we are not challenging ourselves to our full potential. And more importantly, we are not achieving the goals and dreams destined for us.

Everything you want in life is just outside your comfort zone.

Like a rubber band, comfort zones expand and shrink, depending on how they are pulled. Have you ever noticed that rubber bands never retain their original shape once they've been pulled and stretched? Its shape becomes larger and larger as it is stretched.

Such is life. As you go outside the box to try and experience new things, as you test the boundaries of your mental and physical strength, your comfort zone expands as well - your mind is a rubber band!

> More than 500 of the most successful people have said their greatest success comes just one step <u>beyond</u> the point at which defeat had overtaken them.
> ~ Napolean Hill, Think and Grow Rich

As you consistently take risk and expand your comfort zone, you slowly become more *comfortable* feeling *uncomfortable*. Most of us subconsciously avoid feeling uncomfortable at all costs – that is a natural and intrinsic quality of our human nature to avoid discomfort and pain.

But I suggest and challenge you to change your mental association with this feeling of being uncomfortable; instead of avoiding it, consider embracing it. At least then you will know you are testing your limits and are challenging your personal boundaries and limitations.

> *You only find your limits by going beyond them.*
> ~Roger Bannister

What would you do right now, if you knew you would not fail? Write it down:

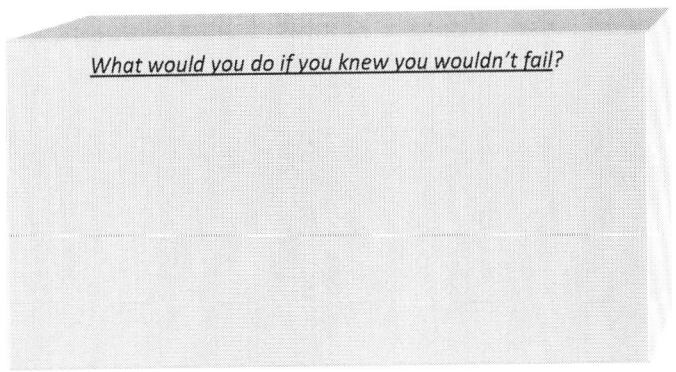

What's keeping you from taking action towards this goal? Is it fear? Perhaps fear has been keeping you in a comfort zone, whether you have realized it or not.

You can accomplish anything you set your mind to. And if fear has been holding you back, one of the first steps you *must* take is to break through your comfort zone.

Associate feeling uncomfortable as a requirement to living your dream and achieving goals. Now that is an incredible feeling! And when you achieve and manifest that goal or intended outcome, you will want to apply this fundamental concept more and more.

It will take effort to change this neuro-association and it most likely will not happen overnight. It will take time. But like a toddler learning to walk, you will have to take baby steps to change this mental focus. And even if you fall down and feel like you can't continue, you have to force yourself to try again and again – and even then again. Remember, it's not how many times you fall, it's how many times you get back up.

Look back on how you learned to ride a bicycle. Did you successfully ride on the first attempt? More than likely, you fell down and probably even hurt yourself. Moreover, you even had training wheels to prepare you for riding on your own.

Look at how you build muscle and become physically healthy. Do you build muscle simply overnight, or does it require mental and physical discipline over a period of time?

You have the power to alter your physical appearance by changing your diet and exercise routine. Granted, some people seem to be more genetically gifted than others in this area, but it is simply fascinating to know we can alter our bodies' physical shape and appearance when we decide to. This process takes time and requires dedication and sacrifice.

I've mentioned only a few simple analogies of how anyone can change an outcome by *thinking differently* and outside the box. We have grown up understanding these concepts and lessons, but yet most people do not apply them in their personal lives. Most of society has no understanding of expanding *comfort zones* and *thinking differently* – that is also why most of society is content with being mediocre. I do no write that statement in a negative tone. My personal definition of mediocre is "status quo," or an acceptance of being average.

There is nothing wrong with being average, but that is not an operational level of living I personally will accept. I do not believe my purpose is to be "average." I choose and aspire every day to live my life exceptionally, with passion and purpose. It's a choice. What will you choose?

****

Are you familiar with the name Roger Bannister?

Roger was an amazing athlete who broke the 4-minute mile record in the mid 1950s. Up until that moment, it was thought humanly impossible that the 4-minute mile record could be attained. Experts claimed this coveted milestone would always remain, and everyone believed it. That is, until Roger Banister.

When Roger broke the 4-minute mile record, he proved it could be done. Within one year following Roger's amazing accomplishment, several other individuals broke the same 4-minute mile record. A year after that, even more. Since then, dozens more.

What was the difference between these two years? Was it technology? Drugs?

Most certainly not. The single reason why others were able to break this record was because they *knew* it could be done. Roger proved to the world that the 4-minute mile was only a mindset. It was a mental limitation and boundary that he believed could be broken through. He *thought differently* and courageously leaped outside of the comfort zone which society established for everyone else.

Wouldn't it be amazing to live daily like Roger Bannister? Imagine for one moment that every limitation and obstacle you hear about or visualize can be broken through. Envision the achievement of breaking through a barrier which everyone else sees except you. Feel the fulfillment of living your dreams before you even embark on the journey towards them.

What limitations have you placed on yourself? What has someone told you could not be done and you believed them? What traditions have you accepted because no one has been willing to think outside the box or comfort zone?

The next time someone tells you that you can't do something or that some achievement cannot be accomplished, I want you to remember Roger Bannister. I want you remember that Roger did what everyone said could *not* be done. And the moment he proved it could be done, he changed history.

So when you hear the phrase, "we've never done it that way" or "that won't work," please smile at that person and say "OK - thank you." Then proudly allow them to watch you do it.

There are hundreds of stories just like Roger Bannister's. In my leadership programs, you have heard me talk about many of these examples.

****

Jack Canfield & Mark Victor Hansen

Who are these two individuals? Most likely, you have either read or heard about their series of books.

Jack Canfield and Mark Victor Hansen are the co-editors for *Chicken Soup for the Soul*, the most successful series of book lines ever published.

However, these books were not successful overnight, and in fact, the publishing of these books was nearly a miracle. What most people do not know is that Jack Canfield and Mark Victor Hansen went to dozens of publishers before someone actually thought their idea would be successful. Meaning, they had dozens of people telling them "No," or that their idea wouldn't work.

But that final publisher said "Yes," and look how successful this series of books has become. And that one "Yes" is what has made all the difference.

What would have happened if Jack and Mark stopped at every time they were told "No?" *Chicken Soup for the Soul* would not exist. But because they were determined and believed in their dream, they knew it was just a matter of time before someone would see the potential in their idea. In fact, they expected publishers to *not* like their idea. So when the doors were shut in their faces, they were not surprised.

An invincible determination can accomplish anything.
~Jack Canfield and Mark Victor Hansen

How many attempts will you take towards your dream, towards an idea that others may or may not believe in? Will you be like Jack Canfield and Mark Hansen, or will you expect the easy route and stop when things get tough?

Remind yourself that by *thinking differently*, you can be like Jack Canfield and Mark Hansen. These two individuals are no better than you or me; they just kept trying and believed in themselves and their product.

How many attempts will you take to live your dream?

****

Michael Jordan

Yes, I am sure you are familiar with this name.

Also known as "MJ," Michael Jordan is one of the best basketball players in history:

>NBA's Most Valuable Player: 5 times
>NBA Finals Most Valuable Player: 6 times
>Member of NBA Championship Team: 6 times
>NBA Scoring titles: 10
>All-Star: 11 times
>Slam-Dunk Champion: 2 times, 1987 and 1988
>Average points per game: 31.5 (NBA record as of 1998)
>Highest points in a regular season game: 69 points
>Number of game winning shots: 25
>Games with 50 points or more scored: 37

But did you know that Michael Jordan was actually cut from his high-school basketball team? Yes, one of the world's best basketball players was once told he wasn't good enough.

But what do you think MJ did when he got home that day after being cut from the team? Play video games? Complain and turn away from the sport he loved? Believe that he wasn't good enough?

Heck no.

The first thing MJ did when he got home was practice. He knew he was better than what the coach thought. In fact, he didn't believe the coach for one second. And for the next year, MJ practiced constantly, shooting free throws and lay ups, getting better and better each day.

And when tryouts occurred, he made the team; in fact, he did amazing. He then played for the University of North Carolina at Chapel Hill; he did amazing there too. Then he played for the NBA. The rest is simply history.

The point of sharing MJ's story is to communicate that achieving dreams and goals takes sacrifice, discipline, sweat and even tears. Nothing worthwhile ever just happens overnight. Yet, we usually want and expect it to.

The reason you and I know about Michael Jordan is because he *thought differently*. He knew he was better than what that high-school coach thought of him. He knew he would break records and be an amazing basketball star. If Michael Jordan believed what the coach initially thought of him, he would not have achieved the records he did and we most likely would not even know his infamous name. What mattered to him was what HE thought of himself, not what anyone thought of him.

Moreover, he used the disbelief from others to actually help him become a better basketball player. I believe "he is, who he is" *because* he was cut from the basketball team. He used that experience to his advantage and, as a result, became a better person.

Do you have the same attitude as Michael Jordan with your goals and aspirations? Do you need someone else's approval to live your dream? Has anyone ever told you that you were not good at something? Did you believe them?

The next time someone doubts you or says that you cannot do something, remember Michael Jordan's story and *think differently*. Smile at them; then proudly let them watch you do it.

Be like Mike.

****

Imagine you are MJ for one moment, and you have the basketball. What are the chances of the ball going into the hoop if you do not shoot it?

<u>ZERO</u> – that's right.

When do not take a shot, ther8e is a 100% chance that the ball will not go in. When you take a shot, at least you have a chance. And in fact, you probably have a good chance of getting the ball in if you actually play basketball. And the more you practice, the better your chances will be. But if you do not shoot the ball, you will never know.

"I've missed more than 9000 shots in my career. I've lost almost 300 games. 26 times, I've been trusted to take the game winning shot and missed. I've failed over and over and over again in my life. And that is why I succeed."
~ Michael Jordan

When you shoot, you at least know if the ball goes in or if you miss. But even if you do miss, then you know if you shot the ball too hard, too soft, too far left or too far right. At least you know how to adapt your strategy for the next shot.

So the more shots you take, the better you will be because you learn from each preceding attempt.

You always miss 100% of the shots you never take –
<u>IN LIFE!</u>

None of us always take the right shots in life; we all make mistakes. But what is important to understand and apply is that mistakes are also lessons of wisdom. This specific theme will be repeated several times throughout this book.

When we have the right attitude, we can learn from our mistakes and become more experienced individuals.

> *When you lose, don't lose the lesson.*
> ~ The Dalai Lama

But yet why are these concepts so difficult to apply in our daily lives? Why do so many of us quit so often or get frustrated when things don't go our way? So many times we expect life to be easy, and when it's not we beat ourselves up. We're much too hard on ourselves.

One of the secrets to actively apply these philosophies is that we must ask ourselves better questions to get the results we want. Meaning, when things don't go our way, instead of asking "what did we do wrong," we should ask "what can I learn from this experience?"

When we're stopped short of our goal for some reason, or when something apparently bad happens to us, instead of asking "why does this always happen to me", replace that with "how does this experience make me a better person?"

It's all a mindset and it takes hard work to live with this philosophy. But believe me, when you apply and live with this approach to goals and dreams, the world and every experience you desire is at your fingertips. You can never lose unless you give up. You can always learn something, even when you don't get your way, but only when you ask yourself the right questions.

Ask yourself a bad question, you will get a bad answer.
Ask yourself a good question, you will get a good answer.

Fulfillment is as simple as understanding and applying this philosophy and approach to life. Again, you can never lose when you ask yourself the right questions.

Whether it's a bad experience at your job, a bad relationship, disappointing feedback you received on something, rejection regarding something you've pursued, etc. – it doesn't matter. Even when bad things happen, you still are a better person as a result when you ask yourself the right questions.

In this chapter, we've reviewed several amazingly famous people: Roger Bannister, Jack Canfield, Mark Victor Hansen and Michael Jordan.

What do all these people have in common?

The commonality that all these examples share is that they *think differently*. Their success is a direct result of their mentality, and their belief system says "never quit – keep trying." All of them consistently asked themselves good questions even when it seemed hopeless. When others would have quit, they kept trying. They believed in their goals, took persistent action, and are remembered greatly for it.

A great many years ago I purchased a fine dictionary.
The first thing I did with it was to turn to the word "impossible,"
and neatly cut it out of the book.
~ Napolean Hill, Think and Grow Rich

Remember, THINK DIFFERENTLY!

NOTES/THOUGHTS ...

I Lived My Dream

A Story of Passion, Persistence and
The Price is Right!

I had religiously watched *The Price Is Right*, television's longest-running game show, for as long as I can remember. Growing up, I was obsessed with the show and planned my lunch around watching it every day. Even at college, I deliberately scheduled my classes around the show. For four years, I never had a college course at the magical hour of 11 a.m., just so I could watch *The Price Is Right* every single day!

During my junior year, I attended a student leadership conference where I met Chris, an eccentric guy with a funny personality. We became instant friends. During one of the conference sessions, we participated in an icebreaker where we had to share something unique about ourselves. When it was his turn, Chris stood up and announced he had just returned from a Spring Break trip where he'd been on the *The Price Is Right* and won a gazebo!

Amazed and envious, I nearly fell off my chair! Chris had no prior knowledge of my obsession with the show. Meeting him felt like a divine sign, and I knew I was destined to be on *The Price Is Right* as well.

At that specific moment, I made the conscious <u>decision</u> to shake hands with Bob Barker and be on *The Price Is Right*. I truly believed and mentally envisioned I would not only be a contestant, but also a winner. Even though I had no idea "how" to get on the show, there was no doubt in my mind that this dream would come true.

Throughout the conference, I questioned Chris about his experience and absorbed the advice he shared about being selected as a contestant. He suggested taking advantage of the time standing in line while waiting to enter the studio. "The secret," he said, "is that the producers scan for contestants before the show even starts – that is how they select 'Contestants Row'."

I learned that potential contestants who obnoxiously stand out or are in large, exuberant groups of people have a better chance of hearing those magical words, "Come on down!"

After learning all this, the "how" of my dream became clear. I was convinced that if I traveled from my home in North Carolina to California and was somehow part of a group, the producers would see the excitement in my eyes and my dream of shaking Bob Barker's hand on *The Price is Right* would manifest.

Since Chris lived in California, he agreed to be the ring leader who would organize my accomplices. We kept in touch, hoping to find an available date where I could drive across the country and enact the plan. Unfortunately, the only date where we could coordinate our adventure was the same date as my own college graduation!

As difficult the decision was, I knew that pursuing my dream of being on *The Price is Right* would be incredibly fulfilling and exciting. Driving across the country and sacrificing my college graduation seemed to make my pursuit even more worthwhile. I decided to go.

While my classmates were preparing to attend graduation, I was preparing to drive to meet my destiny.

Three long days after leaving North Carolina, I finally arrived in Los Angeles and met Chris and his friends. The next morning our caravan headed out towards *The Price is Right* studio parking lot. My anticipation energized us all. As we pulled into the parking lot, I was reminded of a movie scene from *National Lampoon's Vacation* – the scene where the Griswalds travel to Wally World only to discover that the amusement park is closed!

The Price is Right parking lot was *E-M-P-T-Y!*

In disbelief, I stumbled from the car and sat on the ground, my stomach threatening to heave up the remnants of my breakfast. A security guard appeared to inform us that Bob Barker was sick and had cancelled the show for the next two weeks. In front of everyone, tears flooded down my face. My graduation ceremony had been sacrificed for nothing.

I had no choice but to drive back home a few days later. Despite my disappointment and shock, my dream of being a contestant was only made stronger through this first failed experience.

I continued to keep in touch with Chris, knowing that I would need his help again. Even as a young college graduate, I understood the most important things in life require belief, dedication, and sacrifice. I still believed; I was dedicated to my goal; and I had already proven that I was willing to make the sacrifice.

About one year later, I called Chris to tell him that I was ready to try again. After picking our date and ordering tickets, I purchased a plane ticket to Los Angeles. Chris was in charge of arranging another energetic group of supporters to go with us.

I arrived to the airport at 11 p.m. and Chris and his friends were waiting to take me straight to CBS television studios. This time the lot was empty because we were the first The *Price is Right* fanatics in line!

Nearly eight hours later, with over 800 other potential contestants behind us, I noticed staff walking through the lines. My moment to convince them to select me had arrived.

When they got to our group, one of the producers asked me, "Where are you all from?"

I inhaled and babbled the 20-second version of my *Price is Right* obsession and life story. The producers laughed, but made no indication of my chances to be called on the show. As they moved onto the other 800 people waiting in line, Chris rolled his eyes and said "Dude, you are weird! I hope they do select you so you can move on with your life."

All I could do now was contain the butterflies in my stomach and wait.

A few hours later we were finally seated in the television studio. I could barely sit still as I waited for the show to begin. As *The Price is Right* theme music started, I prayed to hear my own name called down to contestant's row.

The first contestant was called. Not me.

Contestant number two was called. Not me again.

With two more contestants to be called, I finally heard those magical words. "Kevin Snyder, Come On Down! You're the next contestant on *The Price Is Right*!"

Yes, I was contestant number 3!

Much about that moment was a blur, but I do recall wildly jumping up and knocking Chris to the floor. My date with destiny and Bob Barker had finally arrived.

I did not win the first prize on contestant's row – I underbid. However on the second item, I placed a near perfect bid on a diamond bracelet and won. After toppling Chris over again in excitement, I ran onstage to Bob, shook his hand, placed my hand on my chest, and enjoyed the surreal moment of my dream coming true.

Onstage, I played "Punch-a-Bunch," a game where I could win prizes and up to $10,000 in cash. I ended up winning all the prizes which resulted in four punches on the money board. Each punch hole contained various amounts of money, and from one of my punches Bob pulled out $5,000! I won BIG!

My total prize winnings were the diamond bracelet, a steam vacuum, a napkin holder, a wicker basket, a milkshake maker and the $5,000!

After celebrating that night with Chris, I reflected on this journey of living my dream.

Although some may call my dream trivial, juvenile, or even crazy, My *Price Is Right* adventure changed my life and continues to impact my life each day. This story is not just about a game show or winning prizes. The message is about taking time to identify passions in life, no matter what they are or how silly they may seem, and then persistently taking action to manifest these desires in our lives.

And even though we may fail during the process, it is the failure and setbacks that teach us the most. Even when an experience is negative, frustrating, and appears to be a major set-back, we must realize that we become better, more experienced and educated people as a result of it.

Whenever I'm feeling overwhelmed or pessimistic, all I need to remember are those magical words, "Kevin Snyder, come on down" and I know all my dreams are attainable. All I need is persistence and faith.

I continue to live my dream now as I speak at college campuses around the country, bringing the message of passion, persistence, and *The Price is Right*. I'll close this story the way I close my presentations with a quote from Thomas Edison." *Our greatest weakness lies in giving up. The most certain way to succeed is always to try just one more time."*

And finally, never forget that famous Bob Barker phrase, "Remember to have your pets spayed and neutered. Goodbye, everybody!"

NOTES/THOUGHTS ...

Passion

*When you have passion for something,
You find a way to make it happen.*
~ Zig Ziglar

This will be my favorite chapter, simply because it discusses a concept which I believe is *the secret for living a fulfilled life* – PASSION.

Passion must be at the root of all we do. If we are not passionate about the activities, organizations and responsibilities we accept and are part of, we will not be successful or feel fulfilled.

Most of us know how to identify and set worthwhile goals. However, have you ever set a goal that eventually becomes less interesting over a period of a few weeks or months? Perhaps you were initially motivated but sooner than later, that motivation died just as quick as it started.

We all have been motivated before to achieve something, and indeed, we were actually interested in it. However, two weeks or two months later we are struggling to push onward and continue our efforts toward accomplishing it.

Being a motivated person is significantly different than being a passionate person. You see, motivation goes away unless we are truly passionate about the goals we envision and spend our time pursuing.

Unlike motivation, passion is a fuel that never runs empty. Pursuing a goal you are passionate about will never be cumbersome or a chore; rather it will be exciting and enjoyable to work toward. The more you pursue it, the more excited and fulfilled you become.

> *All achievement must begin with an intense, burning desire and passion for something definite.*
> ~ Napolean Hill, Think and Grow Rich

Goals we are passionate about are simply glorious to pursue. Yet why do we *not* invest our time, talent, and energies toward goals we are truly passionate about? How many hours of the day do you honestly spend doing something you love, something you are passionate about? Unfortunately, if you are like most people, you will spend very little time, if any at all.

Is what you spend most of your time doing worthwhile and something you are truly passionate about?

If you took a journal for one week, or even one day, you would easily identify what you spend most of your time doing. Moreover, I bet you would be shocked at how much of your day is spent just being busy. More importantly, you will see how little time you invest on yourself and doing things you are truly passionate about.

Unfortunately, most people are never challenged to ask themselves these questions. Most likely because we would not want to agree with, or realize, the alarming answers. Most of us are so busy with creating daily and weekly checklists that we associate being extremely "busy" the same as being productive and effective. But being busy is just that – *only busy*. And being busy means that you have *less time* to spend on things you truly care and are passionate about.

The only thing "busy people" have truly accomplished is transforming themselves into hamsters on a wheel. The hamster appears so amazingly busy as it moves that wheel so quickly, yet where is it actually going?

The hamster goes absolutely *nowhere*.

We've all felt like a hamster at times. It is natural for us to become so busy that we lose sight of what is most important in our lives. In fact, there might be days and weeks when we feel as if we do not have a choice regarding what we spend our time doing. But it's during these moments and days when we must say "no" to accepting additional frivolous tasks. It is during these times when we must <u>refuse to not have control</u> over own lives.

Do not give control of your life to something greater than you and what you believe in. Is your busy schedule truly more important than your health and well-being, your family and your success?

I challenge you to make time each day for something you are passionate about. You might even have to schedule this allotted time but when you do, know that it is *your time* and no one else's. Even the "busiest" people have 15-30 minutes each day to spend on themselves. It's just a matter of the choices we make.

Life is all about choices – what will you choose? To simply be busy all the time, or will you choose to be fulfilled and passionate?

Each day, you should spend 15-30 minutes on something you are interested in and passionate about.

More frequently than not, I have people ask me "what if you're not passionate about something – how can you be?"

I then work with them to identify their interests and what they enjoy spending time on. Together, we usually find that they don't spend time enough time on themselves, their simplest pleasures and even their interests. They are those "busy people" I have been referring to. They have not taken control of their life – rather, it has taken control of them.

Taking time for you each day is not selfish. You might say to yourself that you have too many responsibilities or make up other reasons why you cannot invest 15-20 minutes on yourself.

What you've done is create a list of EXCUSES, and excuses are the number one reason why most people will never live their dream and be able to look back upon life with no regret.

What are the excuses <u>you</u> typically make for why you cannot do something? If you are investing time on things you're not passionate about, you most certainly are making excuses, whether you realize it, consciously or not.

<u>The top excuses are below</u>:
I don't have time.
I don't have enough money.
I have kids and a family that need my attention.
I'm overweight.
I'm not strong enough.
I'm too old.
I'm too young.

Whatever the excuse you use, *you're right*! When you identify reasons why you *cannot* do something, that's what your focus will surely be on. Your thoughts will perpetuate that reality.

Whether you think you can or cannot, you're right.

What you focus on expands. And when you tell yourself you can or cannot do something, you will attract those exact circumstances. Your life is consistently made up of the orders you give it. We will revisit this philosophy several times.

For example, what does a restaurant server bring to your table when you order a Coke, chicken sandwich and french fries? They bring you exactly what you order, and if they brought you something different, you would send it back.

Such is life – we make mental orders to ourselves dozens, if not hundreds, of times each day. We tell ourselves we can or cannot do something, but all we've done is make an order for our own life. Tell yourself you don't have time; you won't. And you certainly won't make time either. Tell yourself you don't have enough money; and you don't. Tell yourself you are too young or too old; you are exactly right.

So why *not* get rid of excuses and spend your mental energy on reasons why you *can do something*, rather than why you cannot? We spend more time and attention on thinking of excuses rather than on finding creative ways to accomplish what we desire.

If you are not used to applying this philosophy, it will require work at first. However, eventually you make this mindset a habitual routine to deal with daily situations. As a result, you will take control of your own life and will become truly a master at what you set your mind to. Utilizing this philosophy and principle is a personal power most will never even understand.

The reason most people settle for mediocrity is that they have chosen never to master something they truly love.
~ Anthony Robbins

****

I believe the secret key to unlocking all life has to offer is understanding PASSION and how it relates to our lives. Everyone has access to this key; in fact, they hold it in their hands each day. Unfortunately, most do not know they hold it so closely, if at all. The *secret* is that it's *not a secret*.

You can lead a more fulfilled, passionate life starting right now – *if* you decide to. Reading the rest of this book won't matter much for you unless you truly have a desire to take advantage of life and what it has to offer.

I acknowledge that we all have different circumstances, and some of us have more "responsibility" than others which might limit how much risk we can take to make a personal, life change. But that does not mean we cannot make a change; rather, it just means that we must consider these "responsibilities" as we move forward toward manifesting those things we are passionate about in our lives. Where some can make a 10 degree change, others can only make a 1-2 degree change. The amount of degree is irrelevant; what matters is the effort and action of simply beginning.

> *Each day, you should spend 15-30 minutes on something you are interested in and passionate about.*

So instead of saying "No, I have too much responsibility," ask yourself "How can I manage my responsibilities and still achieve my desires?" When you ask yourself "how," it eliminates the excuses and opens our mind to creatively find the answers.

Always ask yourself "how."

NOTES/THOUGHTS ...

Lessons of Wisdom

Our greatest mistakes can be our greatest lessons.

We all make mistakes – no one is perfect. In fact, acknowledging and learning from our mistakes builds moral character, fosters integrity, and redirects our focus in a positive manner.

It's when we choose *not* to learn from our mistakes when we lose the lesson that life offers to teach us. Even when you lose, don't lose the lesson.

****

When I was a high school senior in North Carolina, I became president of a student organization called *Knightsounds*, which was a show choir. Each year, our group traveled to Disney World in Orlando, Florida, to compete in a nation-wide tournament competition.

My mother was also a Math teacher at my high school and she was a chaperone on this same trip.

During the tournament in Orlando that particular year, I became especially fond of a special girl in the organization. We spent most our free time together in the same group of friends.

While walking around the shops at Disney on the first day, I immediately noticed that this group of "friends" was shoplifting at nearly every store we visited – and none of them ever got caught. What disappointed me even more was that the girl I liked was also stealing items.

After the first day, I decided to simply keep my mouth shut and not say a word to anyone. I certainly did not want to get the group I was with, especially the girl I liked, in trouble. And I certainly did not want to say anything to my group of "friends", worrying they would unwelcome me from hanging around with them.

At the end of the third and final day of the competition, we were given several hours of free time before needing to be back on the bus for departure. Of course, I spent this time with the girl I liked and her group of friends.

While in the final shop before heading back toward the bus, I bought a Disney t-shirt. I then waited outside for my group for several minutes. When I returned inside to the store to find out what was taking so long, I found them shoplifting again.

But this time, I became tempted to impress and show them I was just as clever as they were. I could also steal a few items with no one noticing. Without even thinking, I looked around, grabbed a hat and put it inside the same bag as the purchased t-shirt.

I looked around again to make sure no one noticed besides the girl I liked, and then walked outside of the store. The second I put one foot outside, a hand grabbed my arm and stopped me. Next thing I saw was a police badge and a tall man who said, "Come with me." My heart skipped a beat and my legs became immediately numb.

The officer led me to the Disney security station where all my personal information was taken and I was fingerprinted. I had never felt so alone in all my life.

****

My mother walked into the security station exactly during my last fingerprint. I had already been crying, but when I saw the shock and disappointment in her eyes, I started bawling again.

The music director was also with my mother, and they introduced themselves to the officer handling my incident. The officer explained to them what had happened, and I affirmed it. The director responded, saying that I was the last person in the group she would ever expect to do such a thing. Even though the officer could visibly observe I was remorseful and distraught, he recommended that I find legal representation – Disney was going to press charges, and rightfully so.

By this time the bus had already been waiting on me for nearly three hours. Because of me, everyone was sitting in the bus, becoming more restless, miserable and angry with each passing moment. When I was finally released, I made the longest walk-of-shame you can imagine – I was so embarrassed to walk on that bus. I just kept my head down in the front seat, sitting next to my mom, and didn't say a word for hours.

When we stopped for gas, most everyone exited the bus to get a drink or snack. I naturally stayed inside the bus, because no one would talk to me. But just when I thought the bus was empty, someone grabbed me and invited me to go inside for a drink. Feeling relieved that at least one person wasn't as angry as I thought, I slowly walked outside.

When I stepped of the bus, I was surprised to find that this person who invited me was someone I didn't even know – her name was Jenny. Jenny briefly said to me that everyone knew that I felt horrible and that my shoplifting attempt was out-of-character. She continued, saying that everyone knew it was the group of friends I was with who were the people who should have been caught. Even though the words she shared felt refreshing and forgiving, it did not excuse the fact that I did what I did, regardless of being caught.

When I got back on the bus with Jenny, she invited me to sit next to her. Reluctantly I did, but we sat there and talked for the next seven hours of the bus ride.

When we finally returned back to the high school parking lot near 7:00 a.m. the next morning, I saw the high school principal standing at the school entrance, not waiting for the bus, but for me. My dad was right behind him, and neither of them were smiling.

Reality was setting in. Whatever punishment I was about to receive, I knew I deserved it. The principal immediately pulled my dad and I inside his office, where I explained what I had done. I do remember them expressing disappointment in me and that this experience had "appeared" to have already taught me a lesson.

The principal suspended me for five days, even though we had less than one month left of school. I don't remember all of the details about being "grounded" at home, but it was a laundry list that disconnected me from the real world for quite some time. I had no car privileges, no phone access, no freedom after school, no television, etc.

I knew I deserved everything though. I was so ashamed and embarrassed of myself and what I had done. More importantly, I had embarrassed my mother as a chaperone and teacher, my family's name, my entire school, and the *Knightsounds* organization. I learned an incredible lesson about ethics, accountability, and the importance of considering consequences before acting.

Those five days I was suspended were tough and I remember being so disappointed in myself. My parents knew I was beating myself up so bad, that they each called me several times a day just to check up on me. After school ended, our driveway would be nearly full of cars from my friends who were also stopping by to check up on me. It was so surprising to have so many visits that I had to ask some of them to leave because I did not want my parents to come home and think I was having a party!
No one from the shoplifting group, including the girl I *had* liked, ever showed up or called me. Not that they had any responsibility for my actions, but I for the first time in my life, I learned a lesson about true friendship, and that you will never lead or follow true friends down the wrong path.

Jenny visited me every day, too.

When I got back to school after five days of suspension, it felt just plain weird. Of course everyone knew what I had done, including teachers and other students I did not even know. To my unhappy surprise, even the school newspaper had an article on my crime.

On the first day back, I asked the *Knightsounds* music director if I could share a few words with the club. I had prepared some remarks that I wanted to communicate to everyone, expressing my deepest apologies and sincere remorse for my selfish behavior. I also volunteered to remove myself from the position as president.

After speaking to them, I do not recall if they were surprised or caught off-guard, but the room was silent. None of my classmates immediately said a word in response.

Finally, a voice in the back of the room said they did not want me to step down as president, that everyone makes mistakes and that I had obviously learned my lesson. The silence that followed validated consensus amongst the group. I was pleasantly shocked.

****

Even though my school problems seemed to be over, the legal problems were just beginning. Disney did press charges and I immediately secured legal representation to determine the best approach for dealing with the situation. I also began community service before the trial even began, to show good faith, commitment, and that I acknowledged my mistake.
The lawyer was eventually able to reduce the charges to a misdemeanor, and since I was only seventeen, my record would not show the arrest. Thankfully, the legal consequences of this experience would not be a permanent scarlet letter on my life; others are not so lucky.

The attorney charged $2,000. Even though I had an excellent neighborhood lawn business, with roughly 20 yards per week, I wanted to make that $2,000 back somehow so that I would never "notice it" missing from my bank account. I felt that earning $2,000 through a second job would help me put the experience behind me more quickly.

I began working as a waiter at Pizza Inn restaurant just down the street. I kept a log during each shift worked, documenting hours worked and tips made. I also organized each dollar bill on my bedroom desk, and the pile of $1's and $5's rose quickly. I averaged over $14 per hour and ended up earning that $2,000 back within the first three months.

Even I was surprised to make that much money so quickly, and frankly, so easily. Not everyone at that restaurant did as well as I did - and I was only temporary.

On the same day when I finally exceeded the $2,000, my dad took me to the bank, where I deposited everything – in cash. I remember the bank teller looking at me quite awkwardly when I handed over $1100 to her just in $1's!

After we deposited the money, my dad took me out for lunch. We talked about how good it felt to feel that my shoplifting experience had finally reached a stage of closure – I felt able to move on. We also talked about the overall experience and what I had learned from it.

As I was explaining some thoughts, it struck me how much I enjoyed being a waiter. When my dad asked when I was going to quit, I replied to him that I was not – I actually enjoyed being a waiter so much that I was going to continue working at the restaurant. Even though some nights were better than others, I always enjoyed working with people and helping to ensure they had a great experience at the restaurant.

For the first time in my life, I realized how important it was for me to work with, and be surrounded by, *people*. Prior to this experience, the only job I ever had was my lawn mowing business, which was a solitary and monotonous job of walking around in circles. The money was incredible, but there was no true fulfillment or interaction with anyone.

In addition to the lawn business, I also found a new serving job at an upscale restaurant across town. I did very well there as well, but most importantly, I looked forward to working each day. It was clearly apparent to me that my personality was designed to work with, and be around, people – that is <u>Lesson #2</u> learned from my shoplifting experience.

<u>Lesson #1</u> was about accountability and responsibility. When you make mistakes, not only acknowledge them, but learn from them. Everyone makes mistakes, but to repeat them is no excuse. Making the same mistake twice or more is a choice that

people make. Let mistakes serve as lessons of wisdom, so that you can learn from them and be a more educated person.

Mistakes are a part of being human. Appreciate your mistakes for what they are: precious life lessons that sometimes can only be learned the hard way.

I learned the hard way about accountability and responsibility – but the important fact is that I learned. And I learned at a time in my life when the consequences would not be as devastating as they would be now. For that I am grateful.

Lesson #3 was a hidden gem – Jenny. She ended up being my high-school sweetheart and we dated for nearly two years. I would not have met her if it were not for the experience. Not only did she appear in my life during an incredibly difficult time, she was there for me when others were not. She accepted my faults and bad judgments, but more importantly, she helped me realize my decision was not reflective of who I was. Rather, it was simply a poor decision I learned from.
Looking back on this experience, I am amazed and grateful to have learned so much. I am a better person as a result of it, but only because I allowed this to be a lesson of wisdom.

Never regret anything that has happened in your life. It cannot be changed, undone or forgotten. Take it as a lesson learned and move on. Run from it or learn from it.

Every failure brings with it the seed of an equivalent success.
~Napolean Hill, Think and Grow Rich

NOTES/THOUGHTS ...

Your Greatest Accomplishment

The things most important to us are also the things we have to work hardest for.

Take a moment to reflect back on your life and identify one of your greatest accomplishments. In other words, identify something personal of which you are most proud.

You might have several experiences or accomplishments; however select the experience most significant and important to you.

Now, write this accomplishment below:

What is one of your greatest accomplishments?

As you remember this accomplishment, ask yourself the following two questions:

Was this accomplishment a result from luck?

Was this accomplishment a result of something easy and overnight?

These are powerful questions, because I strongly believe, without even knowing *you* that the accomplishment you identified involved sacrifice, hard work, and dedication. I also believe it was a direct result of significant effort over a long period of time and was *not* a result of something that simply happened to you overnight.

You have just realized one of the most important lessons of living a fulfilled life. Our greatest accomplishments do *not* result from luck, being in the right place at the right time, or knowing the "right" person. Rather, our proudest experiences are a result of us sacrificing for what we desire most and taking action persistently over a period of time.

> *The things most important to us are also the things we have to work hardest for.*

However, what does our fast-paced culture want us to think?

Our societal concepts of instant coffee and *instant success* portray an image that we should not necessarily have to work hard to achieve our dreams and that obstacles should be easy to overcome. Society makes most of us feel that if we encounter obstacles, we are on the wrong track and will be criticized. We have become afraid of failure, and its this fear of failure that many times is stronger than our desire for success!

However, this inaccurate portrayal is a backwards image of what is truly most important. And as a result we get caught in the rat race of trying to live a fast-paced, easy and "safe" life void of failure and obstacles.

Fear is nothing but a state of mind, and it is the failure and setbacks we can learn the most from. Our mistakes serve as lessons of wisdom, <u>but only when we ask ourselves the right questions.</u>

Even during an experience that is seemingly negative, frustrating, and appears to be a major set-back, know that you are a better person as a result of it, but only <u>when you ask yourself the right questions</u>.

It is during this time when you must ask yourself the following:

What can I learn from this situation?

*How does this experience make me
a better person?*

When we ask ourselves the right questions, we find the right answers. The following phrase sums it perfectly:

You get what you focus on.

Think of your mind as a fertile soil and your thoughts as seeds being planted. When we allow bad thoughts to consume our minds, we are subconsciously planting bad seeds as well. And as a result, these bad seeds grow into large plants.

Bad seeds = Bad thoughts.

In contrast, what grows in your mind when you plant good thoughts? The results are that these good seeds grow in your mind, and they become large plants as well.

Good seeds = Good thoughts.

Either way, your thinking is a result of what you focus on. And clearly with this example, you reap what you sow!

Dreams are the seedlings of reality.
~ Napolean Hill, Think and Grow Rich

What we must do in every situation is ask ourselves the "right questions" to get the "right answers." When we focus on what we can learn in any situation, especially in unfortunate circumstances, we become more in control of our own life and our destiny. We become powerful and can take advantage of any situation we encounter. Minor setbacks and obstacles become enormous building blocks that help lead us to our goals even faster. Devastating experiences can teach us amazing life lessons *if and when* we ask ourselves the right questions.

> *What can I learn from this situation?*
>
> *How does this experience make me a better person?*
>
> *How does this experience make me a better leader?*

Again, when we ask ourselves the right questions, we get the right answers. The power of your mental focus will dictate how you feel. And how you feel dictates how you act. So focus on the positive, even when it seems invisible, and you will find it. Again, learn from your mistakes because they can serve as lessons of wisdom. No one is ever defeated until they accept it as reality.

Remind yourself of your greatest accomplishments often, especially when you encounter obstacles and frustrations along the journey of pursuing your goal. They will be there – expect them.

NOTES/THOUGHTS ...

The Power of Choice

You are not <u>what</u> you think you are;
rather, what you <u>think</u>, you are.
~ Ancient Proverb

I had a good childhood, growing up in North Carolina with a brother, sister, and two great parents. I played sports, was good in school, and was even active in the community at an early age.

I have a vivid memory of sixth grade, having lots of friends and "going with" several girls. In fact, sixth grade was more fun than educational for me. My parents had to limit the number of phone calls I received at night, and they ordered a second phone line just because I was on the phone, constantly.

In seventh grade, I dated "Crystal" and truly felt junior high love for the first time. In fact, I liked Crystal so much that I wrote "I Love Crystal" on my blue Chucks shoes and on my desk in each class.

We had been dating for six months, which in seventh-grade years is equivalent to a lifetime, when one day she broke up with me in the cafeteria during lunch. I was devastated and remember crying in front of all my friends; obviously our breakup took me by surprise.

The next day during lunch, I saw her holding hands with my best friend.

I felt like I was not good enough for her. I remember wanting to be different, so that she might like me again. For the first time in my life, I faced a significant amount of rejection. And this was only the beginning.

For the next several weeks, I faced even more rejection and change. My popularity seemed to diminish and phone calls at night almost stopped. All of a sudden, I wasn't one of the coolest kids in school anymore. Moreover, I got cut from the soccer team, a sport I loved and had played my entire life. None of this made sense to me, but my life had changed suddenly and drastically, and outside of my control.

A few weeks later, I saw Crystal again at a friend's birthday party. As we were talking, she used her index finger to touch my stomach. Her exact words were, "gaining a little bit of weight aren't we?" Her comment stuck to me and my mind kept repeating those words over and over. Maybe if I lost some weight she would like me again? Maybe if I lost some weight, I would be more popular again? Maybe my weight was a factor in me being cut from the soccer team? I became convinced that my weight was the major source of rejection in all areas and that I had to make a change.

Before I continue, I must acknowledge that I was not the thinnest kid in school, nor was I the fattest. My pictures below show I looked quite 'normal' like the average kid.

Nevertheless, losing weight became a central focus point for me, and I assumed it would help me gain control back in my life.

I tried to diet, but I just was not successful at it. I would eat the wrong foods at the wrong times and my focus was not a healthy lifestyle. For about six months, I went back and forth, losing and gaining about ten-fifteen pounds each time.

I then tried out for the junior high wrestling team. I was pretty good in my weight class of 110 lbs, but most of what I learned during that wrestling season was self-control and how to diet and control my weight. I mastered the ability to manage weight before wrestling matches by eating, not eating, exercising, or not exercising. As a result, my weight consistently remained just under 110.

Then, just before the season was over, I decided to lose weight again, hoping to look and feel better about myself. By this time, losing weight was something I knew I could accomplish.

I remember losing 5-10 lbs and feeling good. At this same time, I received compliments from people that I looked great. Even Crystal commented that I looked good one day. I associated my weight with everything: popularity, Crystal liking me, and feeling good about myself.

I convinced myself that I needed to lose more weight in order to feel even better and get more attention. This is when my disordered behavior began. I would skip meals, exercise continuously at odd times of the day, isolate myself from friends, etc. What started as dieting, led into a preoccupation with food and exercise, which led into self esteem and body image problems, which led into my eating disorder.

The next several months were very dark. I do not remember much at all, other than exercising and drinking lots of diet soda. One of my habits would be to only eat at dinner, so that my family would see me eating. Obviously, they did not know that was the only meal I had the entire day. I would also run and exercise before my parents even woke up in the morning. This dark spiral progressively continued before anyone really knew what was going on, including me.

My mother recalls seeing me from a distance at church, yet not even recognizing me because I was so skinny. It was at this moment where she acknowledged I had lost too much weight. My mom and dad connected the dots.

During school that very next day, my mom came to school and had me sent to the principal's office. I remember this vividly – it was 3rd period Algebra and all my classmates thought I was getting in trouble.

I was surprised to see my mom when I arrived at the office. She had come to take me to the doctor and she assumed I would be extremely angry. But surprisingly enough she recalls me not saying a word, but rather looking at her with eyes of relief.

Below is picture of me that same week, during our annual yearbook photo.

Kevin Snyder, 7th grade picture

At the doctor, I weighed 76 lbs - 34 lbs lighter than six months prior. My pulse was 49 and the doctor was extremely worried.

The doctor asked if I had ever heard of "Anorexia Nervosa." I had not, but when he diagnosed me with this eating disorder, it didn't sound too good. I felt very confused. Everything in my life was confusing and seemed severely out of control.

The doctor then informed my mother, with me standing next to her, that I needed to be admitted into a hospital immediately for treatment. The doctor emphatically stressed that my body could not lose another ounce, and that if I did lose more weight, I was risking severe long-term complications, if not death.

Hearing this, I told my mom I was not going to some hospital. If I did, all my friends would know I had some sort of "problem." Ironically, all anyone had to do was look at me to know I was emaciated. Clearly I was in denial.

While the doctor and my parents looked for hospitals that could treat me, I was allowed to be at home as long as I gained weight and began treatments. This is when my battle started.

Being forced to gain weight was completely against the lifestyle I had developed. Even grasping the severity of my condition, I still did not recognize the importance of eating food – I was terrified of calories and the mental image of putting any "fat" back on my body was horrifying.

Several years later, my dad informed me of a conversation he had with me. He remembered asking me what it was about food that made me so scared. He vividly remembered my response, saying that eating food was the equivalent of someone pushing me into a water tank full of sharks.

My life continued to spiral out of control as I was forced to eat and begin the treatment process. Every day after school my mom would pick me up and take me to psychologists, psychiatrists, nutritionists, weigh-ins at the doctor's office, and occasionally other doctors that wanted to study my rare condition. How my mother had time for this I still do not know, but she taxied me around every afternoon after school. We usually would not get home until right before dinner - this was my life for about six months. Doctors, doctors, weigh-ins, doctors ...

In the meantime, there were no hospitals available to me. There were eating disorder centers for females, but not males. There were clinics for adults but not adolescents. There were centers for juveniles with mixed problems, but none were focused on eating disorders. Being a male, juvenile anorexic, my condition did not fit in any of these places, so I continued being treated while at home.

I still don't remember much during this dark time of my life. Maybe my subconscious did not want me to remember, or maybe my body and mind just shut down, like animals during hibernation. I do know I was miserable and depressed, though.

For the first several weeks, my psychologist sessions were completely silent. I would sit there staring at the floor, feeling that the counselor was a waste of my time. I would not say a word, and the counselor would let me sit there, occasionally asking me a question every fifteen minutes or so, hoping to spark some sort of conversation.

The weigh-ins at the doctor's office were even more difficult. After all, I was supposed to be gaining weight. If at any time my weight dropped, the doctor threatened to find a treatment facility in another state. I did not want that, and I remember one time drinking nearly a full gallon of water just before a weigh-in. I knew I was a few pounds lighter that day and drinking that much water made my stomach almost burst. But I could not allow the doctor to catch me at a lighter weight.

Finally, I broke down during one of my counseling sessions. I remember asking how long I would have to keep coming because all I wanted was to be "normal" again. I didn't feel normal coming to a psychologist – every time I went reminded me I had a problem. My psychologist didn't give me a direct answer, but it was the first time she and I had spoken in weeks.

Then, on the way home that same day, I opened up the side door of the van going 55 mph and put one foot out, preparing to jump. I was so depressed and frustrated that I just wanted to end it all.

I heard my mom scream, and the sound of her voice comforted me enough to get back inside and shut the car door. I don't know if I actually would have jumped out that day, but I sure came close. I could not sleep that same night, as usual. In fact, during this whole dark period I had insomnia, sleeping maybe two-three hours a night. Routinely, I would go to bed near midnight but my mind would be racing with all sorts of issues like exercising, foods to eat the next day, foods not to eat, fat on my body, and more exercise.

But this one particular night changed everything. My mom heard me crying in bed at about 2 a.m. She walked into my room and sat down on my bed. I cried even more. All she said was, "You're going to get better, Kevin." I remember replying, "I can't go on like this. I hate my life – I just want to be normal again."

We both cried for a few more minutes and then I fell asleep.

That particular day was the most important day of my life. I hit rock bottom. After finally having a conversation with my psychologist, nearly committing suicide, and emotionally breaking down with my mother, I made a conscious choice to get healthy. And by finally making a decision to take back control of my life, I slowly began to heal.

You see, I was not going to get better until I made the choice to do so. That is what this chapter is all about:

The Power of Choice

I remember waking up the next morning feeling better than I had in months. I still did my normal routine of exercising before and after breakfast, but I felt motivated to get healthy again.

I still struggled with food, but I knew that gaining weight was the only way I could get back to a normal life. I changed my neuro-association with food, meaning I proactively changed my mental association of food from fear to being healthy and normal. Food was no longer the enemy – it was part of the equation to get me better.

Over the next several months, I gained about ½ lb each week. I continued exercising, but at least I knew I was trying to put the weight back on in the right places.

Since my weight had risen to about 85 lbs, I told the doctor I wanted to wrestle again. Even though he was proud of me for gaining almost 10 lbs, he denied my request. However, he and my mom both agreed that if I got to 90 lbs, then I would have approval to join the wrestling team, whose season had already started.

Gaining just enough weight to be back on the wrestling team became my goal. In fact, it became my obsession, and I gained those remaining five pounds in two weeks. When I went back to the doctor, he wrote an approval note to my wrestling coach. I went to practice the next day and joined the ninety pound weight class.

There were three other guys in my weight class, so I had to beat them in order to start on the team. Within the next week, I wrestled them all during practice – and beat them. I was the starter for the 90 lb weight class at the match the following week!

My mom and dad were extremely happy for me – they were also shocked. Even for me, this experience was surreal. I had set my goal to wrestle again, and here I was better than ever. With all the exercise I had been doing, I was in perfect shape.

The next wrestling match was against our arch rival school. It was a big match and the gym was packed full of people. My mom and dad both came to see me perform. I could tell they were very proud of me.

To many people's surprise, I won my match! I didn't pin him, but I did beat him by points. When I got off the mat, my coach hugged me and told me I had just beaten an undefeated wrestler. I did not know he was undefeated!

The night before this match, the coach had actually called my parents at home and told them I was wrestling the best wrestler in the conference. He wanted my parents to be prepared, because even he didn't expect me to win.

I dominated every remaining match that season, being undefeated and even winning the conference championship, earning a gold medal. I even went further to the state competition and got a third place award in the tournament.

Wrestling gave me a positive focus and was an activity I looked forward to each day. I truly believe it distracted my focus from food and helped me work towards becoming a "normal" kid again.

We all need a goal to work toward and something in our lives that challenges us.

****

My recovery continued to be an uphill battle, but I recognized improvement each week. Some days were better than others, but most days were good. My life finally seemed back in control.

As I got older, I wanted to forget this chapter of my life. Remembering anorexia was not an experience I was proud of. It wasn't until I began motivational speaking that I realized how my story could help others.

After my leadership presentations, I talk with members of the audience. I have been amazed at how many people open up to me about their personal struggles and how they feel my presentations help them feel empowered to make conscious changes in their lives. I have been even more amazed at how many people tell me they are struggling with an eating disorder, or know someone who is.

I believe my story will help others and bring comfort to them by knowing they are not alone. I believe my story will help impact someone else's life and will model a pathway towards healing and improvement. If I beat the disease, surely others can as well.

For those of you who might be struggling with an eating disorder, please talk with someone. Make the choice to get better and become healthy. No one can do it for you, though. You may have to be like me and hit rock bottom first before you acknowledge the severity of your condition.

I was lucky – I got help before it was too late. Looking back, I was about five pounds from death. If my mom had not taken me to the doctor that day during school, I might have died, or would at least have serious long-term health complications. I certainly would not have stopped the cycle myself.

I was so depressed that I did not even recognize the dark depression I was in. My life had spiraled out of control.

But my spiral was stopped because someone else stepped in. And I eventually began the healing process once I made the conscious choice to not accept living a life I hated. I was reborn when I understood <u>the power of choice</u>. And I thank God that it was not too late.

I also believe that wrestling played a critical role in my recovery. To me it was more than just a sport. Wrestling was symbolic of the importance for goal setting. It was reflective of my desire to get healthy and I gave it 110%. When I conquered wrestling, I conquered anorexia. When I was awarded the gold medal at the conference tournament, I was awarded the gold medal for beating anorexia.

I am not a doctor, and I am most certainly not a medical expert on eating disorders. However, I am an expert on the struggles I endured, my survival, my recovery and how I can make reason of my life experience.

I do not agree with the popular phrase, "Things happen for a reason." Rather, I prefer "You have to make reason out of the things that happen."

****

Anorexia Nervosa, along with all eating disorders, is a serious disease – studies have found that complications from eating disorders kill up to nearly 20% of those diagnosed. Eating disorders are also the third most chronic illness amongst adolescent women.

People can and do recover from eating disorders. If you or someone you know is struggling with anorexia, help them. Talk to them and do all you can to get them professional help. The longer the symptoms are ignored or denied, the more difficult recovery will be.

For more information about identifying eating disorders, prevention and how you can help, please visit:

www.mentalhealth.samhsa.gov
www.nami.org
www.emedicinehealth.com
www.edreferral.com

Healthy bodies come in all shapes and sizes. We don't need to change our bodies, we need to change our attitudes.

NOTES/THOUGHTS ...

The Secret

Imagination is the preview to life's coming attractions.
~ Albert Einstein

Have you heard of the new phenomena called *The Secret*? Oprah and Larry King know about it – in fact, both have invested two entire talk shows on this films philosophy. In only its first six months of release, *The Secret* was so successful that many experts were already projecting it to be the most successful personal development program in history. Now, you too can know *The Secret*, but only when you buy it in DVD, soundtrack CD, or book.

Still intrigued to know what *The Secret* is? I wish I could share it with you but unfortunately I can't, because after all, it's a secret.

Actually, not only will I share with you some of the philosophy explained in *The Secret*, I will share more. I will introduce my interpretation of how it will change your life once it is understood and applied.

What is *The Secret*?

The creator of *The Secret* has based its concept primarily upon the Law of Attraction, which she describes as a universal law suggesting that *like attracts like*. Everything in the world, or universe as she describes, is comprised of energy, and this energy attracts *like* energy. For example, as we think good thoughts and feel good, we resultantly attract more of these good things into our lives. The same result happens when we think and focus on negative thoughts and feelings; we attract more of these negative circumstances into our lives as well. So in its simplicity, *The Secret* says you get what you focus on, good or bad. Sound familiar?

The Secret has people talking, as if it were a discovery just found in a deep abyss. In reality, though, its principles can also be found in most teachings of any past or present inspirational speaker, success coach, or motivational author. For example, Anthony Robbins, Norman Vincent Peale, Wayne Dyer, and Zig Ziglar all have expressed and taught a concurring belief system that explains (1) when we know what we want, (2) are focused, committed, and passionate about it truly happening, (3) take persistent action toward this goal, (4) then we will manifest our desires.

So as you might be able to sense from my interpretation of *The Secret*, I do not consider this philosophy such a secret. However, I do validate its intentional, *brilliantly marketed,* and well-articulated message that challenges us to awaken and bring about the personal power that already lies within each of us. Its concept is much more than positive thinking; it is positive *believing*.

> *Our brains become magnetized with the dominating thoughts which we hold in our minds. These "magnets" attract to us the forces, the people, the circumstances of life which harmonize with the nature of our dominating thoughts.*
> ~ Napolean Hill, Think and Grow Rich

This personal power *should be* awakened to dynamically impact everything in our existence. At a time in our fast-paced, technological society when we are conditioned to expect near-perfection and instant success, we have to be frequently reminded that *the things most important to us are also the things we have to work so hard for*.

Applying *The Secret*

It might be hard to agree with or understand, but the philosophy shared in *The Secret* should challenge each of us to identify and awaken forgotten dreams and goals we have not pursued or believed possible. Our greatest dreams cannot manifest in our life until we invite them. Remember again your proudest accomplishment. Did this happen by accident or was it a result of belief, persistent action, and overcoming obstacles? Until you visualize the dream and goal in your mind, you cannot manifest its potential in your life.

Identify a personal or professional goal and desire you are passionate about, within or outside of your "day-time job," and have this goal be as extreme and ridiculous as you can possibly imagine. Moreover, this has to be a goal you truly desire, and more importantly, a goal you truly believe in and are passionate about. Do not focus on "how" you will manifest this goal in your life. The "how" will show up, but only *if* you truly believe in it first.

As I paraphrase what *Chicken Soup for the Soul* co-author Jack Canfield says in *The Secret*, you should equate the "how" of your goals with driving your car during the night. When you drive at night, your headlights only show you 200 feet in front of the car. Yet you can drive from California to New York by only seeing every 200 feet, as long as you have faith to continue driving.

Again, do not focus on or wait for the plan or "how" to achieve your identified goal, the "how" will become more clear as you focus on it, believe in it and take those first steps toward pursuing it. Your subconscious and conscious mind will bring it to you.

Write your desire below.

List here a goal you are passionate about and want to see manifest in your life:

Now that you have identified what your goal is, begin to visualize yourself already accomplishing and receiving it. Focus on it already in your life.

Close your eyes and actually visualize this goal and desire in your life.

Then, just as the Law of Attraction promises, you begin to attract this outcome like a magnet, and it will manifest in your life.

This is the part of dream visualization that most people do not understand. And because they do not understand it, they never attract its full potential to their life.

If you have visualized your desire correctly and without distraction, your chest should be full of energy. This is the emotion and state of mind you must capture as you begin to take action toward this goal. Feel this as often as possible.

Try this exercise repeatedly in a setting where you can truly focus. Results may or may not happen overnight, but you will feel and see progress eventually. Then, repeat this exercise with every desire you identify.

As we utilize our ability to intentionally focus on unwavering success and continually improving upon what works well, we become incredibly powerful people. Our energy becomes magnetic and attracts positive circumstances. We exercise the personal power within our mind and manifest the goals in our personal and professional lives.

Disclaimer: The law of attraction only works for people who believe it will.

NOTES/THOUGHTS ...

More to The Secret

What you think about, you bring about.
~ Chuck Danes

As often as I share the philosophy behind *The Secret*, I am routinely confronted by people who say it will not work, that it is unrealistic and naïve to believe you can literally attract circumstances in your life. In response to them, I usually just smile. Then I ask if they have ever heard of a Vision Board. Most of them have not.

I then share my amazing story of when I put *The Secret* to the "test," and why I am so dedicated to now live by its principles on a daily basis. Because you see, before my test, I had doubts about the Law of Attraction myself. I felt, and still do, that persistent action is required to achieve goals and dreams, in addition to believing in passionate goals and envisioning success. You cannot just sit back, dream big thoughts, and expect these things to come into your life. Just doing that is unrealistic, lazy, and simply naïve.

Many people live by *The Secret* but just don't know it – remember *The Secret* really is not a secret. It has just been brilliantly packaged so anyone can understand and learn from it. Even when Oprah Winfrey had several of the main philosophers on her show, she admitted that she had always lived by the same philosophy, but that she did not know it was a secret!

I feel the same, but I never acknowledged the importance of the visualization process in achieving my goals. Meaning, I never recognized that perhaps the "thought" process was just as important as the "action" process. That the equation for achieving extreme levels of success was based on these two factors, interdependently.

> *Anything the mind can believe, it can conceive.*
> ~Thomas Edison

> *All goals in life must first begin with a dream.*
> ~ Walt Disney

Think about my *Price is Right* story (Chapter 2). Before I ever met Bob Barker and was a contestant on the show, I knew without any doubt, that I would be shaking hands with him on stage, on national television. I had a mental image so strongly vivid that I envisioned myself with him before it ever happened. Was it luck that I actually did get called down to contestants row? Or perhaps was it the Law of Attraction at work in my life?

Regardless, I lived my dream despite hurdles and obstacles along the way. But as I remembered this experience, it struck me that perhaps something greater than I was at work to manifest that reality in my life. With *The Secret* fresh in my mind, I decided to create a Vision Board and set more goals that were just as extreme, if not more so, than my dream of being on *The Price is Right*!
The Secret introduces the powerful concept of a Vision Board, which is literally a poster pasted with your desires, goals and dreams. It is symbolic of what you truly want in your life, and what you passionately believe you are attracting to you.

My Vision Board was, and still is, very simple. At this particular time, I had clippings of items from magazines and phrases I typed myself, all cut and pasted onto a fluorescent orange poster board. My board was reflective of my true desires and was comprised of things I honestly saw myself achieving. That is Rule #1 with your Vision Board; you must passionately believe in everything you put on there.

On my board, just some of the items I put on there were a new job, the salary I was going to make, a partnership with a speaking agency, a doctorate degree "paid for," a dog leash invention, and <u>this book</u>.

The important reminder to know about the goals mentioned above is that they were only "ideas" at the time I put them on my Vision Board. I believed in them and saw them in my life, but they were only dreams in my mind. And some of them, quite frankly, were ridiculous. I had no clue "how" they were going to arrive into my life, but I believed in them.

Now, only ten months later, I am reporting to you that everything mentioned has been achieved, or is in full process of being manifested in my life. It is beyond amazing – let me explain.

Not only did I (1) accept a new dream job, (2) receive a salary within $1,000 of what was on my Vision Board, but (3) I am now a professional speaker with the CAMPUSPEAK team and have spoken to over 300 audiences. Moreover, (4) a doctorate program was created at a nearby university. I applied, was accepted, and the classes were even moved to the same campus where I had worked. Amazingly, I was also approached and told that this doctorate program would be "paid for."

So my "test" to see if the Vision Board concept truly worked proved true to me. It was actually fun to play around and treat this concept like a game I knew I would win.

But I am not done yet – the best example is still to come.

For years, I have an idea about a dog leash invention. When I had two puppies, Guinness and Snuka, I would take them for walks, only to be frustrated that their leash lines would consistently become tangled. I would spend nearly half the time during our walks untangling their leash lines.

I began shopping around for a dual, retractable leash that would solve my problem. Unfortunately, I could not find a retractable product out on the market designed for walking two dogs. I went to all the retail pet stores, veterinarians, online stores and more. But I found nothing close to my idea.

Then, the idea hit me to <u>invent</u> the product I was looking for.

I started my invention adventure by doing research on the concept of multi-dog pet leashes. I spent five entire days on the Internet and visiting pet stores, trying to determine if my pet leash product already existed. After nearly clicking to end of the Internet and traveling over two hundred miles, I felt confident that my idea did *not* exist. I could not find any products even comparable.

But even though my idea was crystal clear in thought, I had no clue how to actually make it. And even though I mentally envisioned the leash functioning and walking two dogs simultaneously, I was absolutely lost when I attempted to describe the component parts that made the leash actually work. The "how" of my leash concept was the obstacle I could not overcome. I became very frustrated.

As a result, my invention was put on hold. Six months later, my idea was still on hold. And even though I thought about it frequently, all I did was *think*! I could never figure out how to actually make the leash. The frustration would always return. Again, the "how" of my idea got in the way.

I also had focused my energy on *not* knowing how to create it, rather than attracting the circumstances to get it created. If only I understood the power of the Law of Attraction then.

One year went by. Then two. Then another. No leash. I always had excuses explaining why the leash would *not* work – I was too busy, patents are too expensive, I do not know how to make it, etc. I was more creative with finding excuses than I was with identifying solutions to my problems.

But when I created my Vision Board, four years after conceiving the leash idea, I made the choice to re-kindle my efforts and pursue the leash idea once again. The difference this time though, was *action* and my focus shifted from reasons why I couldn't make it, to reasons why I could.

With the Law of Attraction fresh in my mind, all my mental energy focused on the invention and creation of the leash. I removed all doubt and all excuses that had been holding me back.

Exactly six days after pasting the phrase, "The No-Tangle! Multi-Retractable Dog Leash," on my Vision Board, a student of mine, (Mike) walked up to me and literally asked if I had ever wanted to invent something. I smiled in utter disbelief. I asked Mike what he was interested in inventing. He replied, saying he didn't have an idea, but that he felt I might.

After a few more questions, it turns out that Mike was one of the best computer design students at the university. He was also an engineering physics major, which means he had the brains and computer skills I had been needing since my invention conception. He was the "how" of my dream.

That very next weekend, Mike and I met. I brought several single retractable leashes with me, just so we could break them apart and study how they were designed.

To my amazement, within 45 minutes we had drafted the leash concept I had envisioned and dreamed about. For four years I procrastinated, but in less than one hour it became a reality. Mike was the missing link that arrived as soon as I decided to become committed to the idea.

The story continues.

The very next weekend, I was at a nearby restaurant with some friends. I was introduced to someone to whom I felt an immediate energy and connection with, and I asked her what type of profession she was in. She replied, "I am a distributor for pet supplies."

I almost fainted. She had no clue I had just invented a newly-designed dog leash. Once Mike and I created the leash, she would be the middle-man to help us sell it.

The story continues.

Two weeks after this remarkable meeting, I received a phone message from a friend who is a flight attendant calling to offer me her "Buddy Pass," which means I can fly stand-by for free, anywhere her airline flies. And when I need to travel to exhibit my dog leash to executives and companies interested in licensing it, I can fly for free.

Again, I could not believe how all this was happening to me. It was as if red carpet was being laid out before my eyes, showing me the way to manifest the leash and become amazingly successful.

"Imagination will often carry us to worlds that never were. But without it we go nowhere."
~ Carl Sagan, American Astronomer and Astrochemist

After four years, I finally made the conscious choice not just to "try" and create the leash, but rather, I made the decision that I would create the leash. I put my focus on the creation of it, versus "how" I was going to create it. And when my focus was clear, so was the path made for me.

I met Mike, then my new pet product distributor friend, then the flight attendant. How did this all happen? Was it coincidence? Was it luck? The Law of Attraction at work?

This leash story is just another surreal and exciting example of how you can make anything happen in your life, as long as you believe in it enough, are passionate enough, and willing to make the choice to see it through.

****

It is simple to create your own Vision Board. What I first want you to do is think of all the things you desire out of life. What is it you are seeking? What is it that would truly make you feel fulfilled? What are your goals? Where do you see yourself in one year? Five years? Ten years?

Once you have taken ten-fifteen minutes to clearly focus and identify and focus on your desires, go ahead and write them in the following box. List everything you want in your life right now:

VISION BOARD

(If you have skipped writing in this space above, you are not following directions! You will not ever understand the power of this exercise until you do it! Now go back and fill in items that you desire and would make you feel fulfilled.)

I assume you have written items on your Vision Board this time! But before we continue, I must stress to you that the items you listed must be goals you believe in and are passionate about. They do not have to be realistic; in fact, I would hope some of them seem ridiculous! However, it is imperative that you believe in them so strongly that you already visualize them in your mind.

There is a difference between wishing for something and being ready to receive it. No one is ready until they believe they can actually acquire it. The state of mind must be belief.
~ Napolean Hill, Think and Grow Rich

Remember, Thomas Edison dreamed of a lamp operated by electricity before he created it. When he put his dream to action, despite 10,000 failures, he persisted until he made it a physical reality! The Wright brothers dreamed of a machine that would fly through the air and despite hundreds of unsuccessful attempts, they finally achieved flight!

You have to be convinced that it is only a matter of time before these items tangibly in your life. If you do not feel this strongly about items on your Vision Board, either believe more strongly in them, or remove them from your Board. The Board will only work if you see these things in your mind first!

Remember, what you think about you bring about.

****

Congratulations! You have just created your first Vision Board! Now either photocopy or rip this Vision Board page out of the book and place it proudly in an area where you will see it daily. This will serve as a reminder to you that you must continue to focus on and make efforts towards achieving the goals you have listed.

You cannot just sit back and expect these goals to manifest in your life. This is where I actually disagree with some philosophers when they describe the Law of Attraction. For this law to work, and for your Vision Board to create abundance for you, your passion for these things must be so strong that it *compels you to take action*. And as you begin making efforts, opportunities and doors will begin opening up for you in areas that you have never seen before.

I would rather be ready for an opportunity and not have one, than to have an opportunity and not be ready.

Remember my Vision Board? I was passionate about everything listed, and opportunities arose where I never even imagined. It was synergetic and like magic! I wish for you the same!

I am proud of you for completing what is most likely your first Vision Board (or at least I hope you did). This was a crucial step for you to begin "playing" with this mentality and approach in life. But this Vision Board is only a "baby" board.

Now, or when you are ready, I want you to make another version that is HUGE! I want you to go buy poster board and cut out phrases and clippings from magazines and newspapers that reflect these same messages on your baby board. You need something you can display with pride! Spend more time creating it than what you did earlier. Be proud of your board - there are no limitations except those we acknowledge. You can create anything which you can imagine.

I have shared a great deal of information with you in this chapter, and perhaps it is overwhelming. Truthfully, I hope it has been! And I hope you are feeling challenged. Because challenges breed change and change breeds growth.

I want you to believe in your goals as much as I do. I want you to feel as fulfilled as I do. I want you to capture this power of your mental focus as much as I have, and I want you to do something with it. Self-mastery is the hardest job you will ever tackle. Once you understand and believe that it works, I want you to it teach someone else.

NOTES

Mastering the Art of Effective Communication

We have two ears and one mouth for a reason.

Communication is the foundation for both success and failure. Research from Fortune 500 companies, CEO's, business owners, and entrepreneurs all support that effective communication is essential. They also share that poor communication is the root of all organizational breakdown.

Communication experts say that roughly ninety percent of communication is nonverbal. Meaning, only ten percent of our communication is actually spoken. If this is the case, then what makes up the ninety percent?

"How" we communicate says so much more than what words come from our mouth. It is our body language when we speak, our facial expressions, the tone in our voice, our posture, our smile, and more. Each of these non-verbal gestures sends and perpetuates a clear message before our words are even heard or understood.

It's not what you say, it's how you say it.

Yet most ineffective communicators do not understand this, let alone utilize this to their advantage. When poor communicators need to communicate, they often do so without understanding that their own body language, vocal tone, and facial expressions are saying so much more. Simply smiling, having a good handshake and good posture says something before even opening ones mouth.

Are you aware of your body language? Were you thinking about body language last time you made a presentation or had to confront a friend? What about your next upcoming presentation or group meeting – will you remember the importance of keeping good eye contact, facial expressions, and posture? Again, remember that 90% of what you say is not even communicated in words; a message is sent by "how" you say it.

The most important thing in communication is to hear what isn't being said.

Most of communication in today's fast-paced society is unspoken, not only because of body language, but also because of technology.

Think for a moment about all the ways you communicate on a daily basis. How often do you write a letter and send it in the mail? I would assume it has been a while, if you can even remember. In fact, the last envelope most people have "snail mailed" was a bill they were paying with check!

Snail mail has been replaced by a plethora of other available communication strategies such as email, text messaging, Facebook, Twitter, LinkedIn, Instagram, other various social media platforms, etc. Think of all the ways you have communicated today alone. Chances are you have utilized several of the methods listed above.

The important concept I want you to acknowledge is that our communication has evolved from face-to-face conversations to computers and/or the Internet. It seems we do not even need face-to-face interactions any longer because everything can be "spoken" electronically. This has made communication more easy and immediate, but has it made communication more effective?

The more we rely on technology to get our message across, the more we "think" we have communicated. However, just because we send an email or a message on Facebook, does that truly ensure effective communication? Of course not.

We have all sent and read emails that become misinterpreted. We have all sent and read emails whose message would have been different if it were spoken face-to-face. In residence halls, in our homes, and in our offices, we routinely text or instant message someone next door, in the next cubicle, or even our own room!

To be effective communicators we must understand that just because we sent a message, such as an email, it does not mean we have "communicated." We cannot rely on technology to substitute for conversations that should be taking place in person. We think we have communicated – but we have not.

The single biggest problem in communication is the illusion that it has taken place.

Have you heard, or even said, any of the following:

You didn't get my email?
We posted the minutes on Blackboard. You didn't read them?
We sent everyone a message on Facebook.
My SPAM blocker must have filtered that message.
Email was down for the day.
I sent you a text about that. You should have checked it.

These are just some of the excuses people commonly share for not receiving messages. I have heard every one of them. Sometimes they are honest; sometimes they are nice little white lies because we know we can blame technology. It frequently doesn't work, yet we rely on it so much.

We depend upon technology so much that we have become passive communicators. We send an email and think it's done, that the issue is handled. The major problem with this approach is that you can never be sure when or if the person actually received the message. There is no reply until it is too late or after a decision has already been made.

So the next time you have something very important to communicate, why not utilize several strategies to ensure the message gets across. More importantly, why not call the person directly? If its business, why not arrange a meeting?

Remember, just because you think you have communicated does not mean you actually have. Your message could have easily gotten lost in process or it could have just as easily never been sent. And when you are face-to-face, do not forget the messages you send by not speaking at all.

Remember, it's not what you say, but how you say it.

NOTES

Gratitude

*Nothing new can come in your life until
you appreciate what you already have.*
~ Michael Beckwith

At the closing of every presentation, I share the following message and give out rocks, which I call my "Gratitude Rocks." Even though you may not have a "Gratitude Rock" with you this moment, I want you to immediately identify something near you that is special. Something that is symbolic to you and will remind you of what I describe below:

Keep this "Gratitude Rock" in a special place, so that every time you see it or touch it, you will be reminded of the many things in your life you can be grateful for. You cannot attract any more into your life until you appreciate what you already have.

Focus on living in abundance and you will attract more of it, because you are powerfully attracting more good things to you. It's the Law of Attraction – you become what you think about most; by your thinking, you attract! Sound familiar?

The greatest teachers and inventors who have ever lived have told us that the Law of Attraction is the most powerful law. What you focus on, you attract to you. This Law responds to your thoughts, both positive and negative. Most people think and focus on what they do *not* want, like problems and debt, for example. Then they wonder why these things keep showing up in their lives over and over again. But when you focus on what you want, what you do not want will go away.

When you become aware of this great law, you become aware of how incredibly powerful you are.

You have the magnetic power to change anything, because you are the one who chooses your thoughts. It is a well-known fact that one believes whatever one repeats to one's self, whether the statement is true or false. We are what we are because of the dominating thoughts which we permit to occupy our mind. If you can think it in your mind, you will manifest it in your life. You have the power to change your life by changing your thoughts and feelings. This is your life, and it's been waiting for you to discover it. You deserve all the good things life has to offer.

If you think you'll lose, you're lost
For out of the world we find,
Success begins with a fellow's will-
It's all in the state of mind.

Life's battles don't always go
To the stronger or faster man,
But soon or late the man who win's
Is the one WHO THINK HE CAN!

~ Napolean Hill, Think and Grow Rich

The Essence of Survival

Every morning in Africa, a lion wakes up. It knows it must run faster than the slowest gazelle, or else it will starve to death.

Every morning in Africa, a gazelle wakes up. It knows it must run faster than the slowest lion or else it will be eaten.

In Africa, it doesn't matter whether you are a lion or gazelle, because the when the sun comes up, you'd better be running.

~ Successories quote

****

This book is about you. This book is about *thinking differently* than most people, and by *thinking differently* you will become magnificently successful and fulfilled. This book is also about identifying the role you choose to play in your own life.

Will you be a lion or will you be a gazelle?

You could be the youngest freshman at a university or rather you could be that fifth-year senior anxiously awaiting to graduate.

You could be the president of an organization or rather you could be that common member holding no official position.

You could be the president/CEO of your own company or rather you could be a great, yet "average" employee, who shows up and does good work.

Again, what role will you play in your own life? That's what you have to figure out.

Every chapter you have read in this book has a message of personal power. The common denominator theme is that passion, commitment, sacrifice, and an unwavering positive attitude can attract everything you want in life.

You deserve everything you have the courage to ask for.

Think differently.

A Wish For Leaders

I sincerely wish you will all have the experience of thinking up a new idea, planning it, organizing it, and following it to completion, and then have it be magnificently successful.

I also hope you'll go through the same process and then have something "bomb out."

I wish you could know how it feels "to run" with all your heart and lose…horribly.

I wish that you could achieve some great good for mankind but have nobody know about it except you.

I wish you could find something so worthwhile that you deem it worthy of investing your life within it.

I hope you become frustrated and challenged enough to begin to push back the very barriers of your own personal limitations.

I hope you make a stupid mistake and get caught red-handed and are big enough to say those magic words: "I was wrong."

I hope you give so much of yourself that some days you wonder, "Is it worth all the effort?"

I wish for you a magnificent obsession that will give you reason for living and purpose and direction and life.

I wish for you the worst kind of criticism for everything you do, because that makes you fight to achieve beyond what you normally would.

I wish for you the experience of leadership

Motivation Matters!

Subscribe to Motivation Matters! and receive a weekly motivational message and quotes! Simply email Kevin@kevincsnyder.com or visit www.kevincsnyder.com to subscribe! Each of the following pages contains sample e-newsletters.

DIAMONDS ARE ONLY MADE BY PRESSURE

Do you know how diamonds are actually formed? Read this; it will change your perception:

The very word diamond is derived from the Greek word adamos, meaning the unconquerable. It is known as one of the strongest and most chemically inert materials known. The diamond is nearly impossible to break & can nearly withstand the attack of any chemical. Interestingly, natural diamonds are produced deep under the earths crust under conditions of high temperature and high pressure.

This story explaining the creation of the diamond should remind us how life's pressure can make us stronger, more beautiful people. We cannot produce diamonds without first understanding our own natural qualities and overcoming life's frustrations. The pressure we experience also creates who are, and who we will become.

Perhaps there is a diamond of opportunity hidden in that difficulty you're experiencing now. It may not become a diamond just yet, but be patient, it is forming within you. The diamond scratches all and is not scratched by any.

Quotes

Somebody is always doing what somebody else said couldn't be done.
~ Author Unknown

In the middle of every difficulty lies opportunity - once discovered, such opportunities are like valuable diamonds hidden in the sand.
~ Albert Einstein

When we long for life without difficulties, remind us that oaks grow strong in contrary winds and diamonds are made under pressure.
~ Author Unknown

THE SEVEN UP'S

1. Wake Up! Decide to have a good day.

2. Dress Up! The best way to dress up is to put on a smile. A smile is an inexpensive way to improve your looks.

3. Shut Up! Say nice things and learn to listen. We have two ears and one mouth for a reason.

4. Stand Up! For what you believe in. Stand for something or you will fall for anything.

5. Look Up! To the Lord, higher power and universe you believe in.

6. Reach Up! For your goals, dreams and aspirations. Expect you will achieve them.

7. Lift Up! Be grateful for what you DO have. Nothing new can come into your life until you appreciate what you already have.

What do you wake up for, dress up for, stand up for, look up toward and lift up?

THE POWER TO REALLY LIVE

I like what Mark Twain said about enthusiasm. When asked the reason for his success, he replied, "I was born excited."

The happiest, most fulfilled and most successful people have discovered the necessity of an enthusiastic approach to living. Thomas Edison was also such a person. He was known for his energy and verve. He eventually acquired 1,093 patents for his inventions, including the electric light bulb, phonograph and motion picture camera. He was known to work tirelessly and joyfully. He seemed to love what he did and pursued it with passion. Others have made more money than Thomas Edison, but none have been more enthusiastic or productive.

Ralph Waldo Emerson once said, "Enthusiasm is one of the most powerful engines of success. When you do a thing, do it with your might. Put your whole soul into it. Stamp it with your own personality. Be active, be energetic, be enthusiastic and faithful, and you will accomplish your object." Enthusiasm is an engine fueled by a love for what we do. It will power us anywhere we want to go and take us places we would never reach without it!

What are you enthusiastic about? What do you desire?

ACHIEVING YOUR DREAMS

It's not what you are that holds you back. It's what you think you're not.
~ Denis Waitley

Those wise words from Denis Waitley probably explain more people's failure to achieve the life they seek than any other quote I'm aware of. What keeps most people from achieving their dreams is that they spend too much time dwelling on their weaknesses and shortcomings instead of focusing on their gifts. And that's significantly due to their self-esteem, or lack thereof. Remember, you get what you focus on. And what you focus on expands.

Quotes

Happiest are the people who give most happiness to others.
~ Dennis Diderot, Philosopher

No one has a right to consume happiness without producing it.
~ Helen Keller, American author and lecturer

Ask not what your country can do for you ... ask what you can do for your country.
~ John F. Kennedy, 35th President of the United States

THE POWER OF GIVING

Ever heard this before: "I gave away what I had, to get what I wanted"? It is so true. But you see, most people focus on the 'get'. I need to 'get this', to 'get that'... no - no - no.
That's the hard way, the slow way. The way to GET is to GIVE. Success in our lives and profession is about service and giving to others. Whatever you want more of, start to give it away.

You want more time?
Volunteer.

You want better knowledge?
Give away some books.

You want better relationships?
Be a great friend.

Want more money?
Donate money to someone who really needs it.

What you sow, you'll reap. What does a farmer do? He plants a seed and a harvest is created. Take an inventory of what you have to give away. What about a smile, insight, time, or money. Stop holding on tight and start opening up and putting yourself in the FLOW of life - giving and receiving. It makes the world go round.

What are your talents, gifts and skills? How do you share them? Do you "give" them away?

HAPPINESS

Happiness can be caught, sought or thought, but never bought; The best way to keep happiness is to share it. Happiness is not created by what happens to us, but by our attitudes toward each happening. It isn't our position but our disposition which makes us happy. Stopping at third base adds nothing to the score. That lucky rabbit's foot didn't work for the rabbit. Even a woodpecker owes his success to the fact that he uses his head.

Anywhere is paradise; it's up to you. Happiness is a slice of life --- buttered. If you think you can or you think you can't... you're right!

Quotes

If you want happiness for an hour - take a nap.
If you want happiness for a day - go fishing.
If you want happiness for a year - inherit a fortune.
If you want happiness for a lifetime - help someone else.
~ Chinese Proverb

You don't have to get it right, you just have to get it going.
~ Mike Litman

The more you seek security, the less of it you have. But the more you seek opportunity, the more likely it is that you will achieve the security that you desire.
~ Brian Tracy

THE ROAD TO SUCCESS IS NOT STRAIGHT

There is a curve called Failure, a loop called Confusion, speed bumps called Friends, red lights called Enemies, exits called Temptation, caution lights called Family & possibly flat tires called Jobs.

But if you have a spare tire called Determination, an engine called Persistence, a map called Passion, insurance called Faith, a driver called Creator, you will arrive at your destination called SUCCESS!

For more information

about Kevin C. Snyder and booking information, please contact:

www.kevincsnyder.com or visit *www.InspirActiveSolutions.com*

InspirActive
Envision • Lead • Achieve

About Inspir-Active Solutions, Inc.:
Inspir-Active Solutions, Inc. specializes in developing custom-based keynotes and leadership development seminars, executive coaching, and other personalized business workshops to ignite employee motivation, enhance leadership training, improve performance and increase bottom-line results. Founded by Dr. Kevin Snyder, the company's focus and mission is to facilitate creative solutions that empower business professionals to vision dynamic goals, persist through barriers and achieve peak performance. Whether you work for a company, supervise employees in the company, or ARE the company, Inspir-Active Solutions, Inc. and its associates will help you 'think outside the box' to manifest extraordinary results.

Clients include both small and large corporations, associations, civic organizations, conference planners, and others who seek a powerful, upbeat, and inspirational keynote speaker, facilitator, and/or executive coach. Presentations are intentionally developed to challenge and inspire companies and agencies to advance their organizations to the next higher level and achieve significant results. Each program is specifically tailored to meet any organization's needs and is designed to provide practical tools, skills and ideas to impact dynamic and positive growth.

Keynote presentations and breakout programs are custom designed. Titles include:
> *Discovering the Secrets to Peak Performance!*
> *Anchor Your Leadership!*
> *Leadership Without Limits: Ultimate Success Formula!*
> *Mastering the Art of Effective Communication*
> *The Power of Now: Leaving a Legacy*

Presentation Topics Covered Can Include:
* Leadership Skills Development
* Goal Setting/Motivation
* Empowerment
* Organizational Leadership
* Communication
* Change Management
* Supervision/Personnel Management
* Obstacle Breakthrough
* Teambuilding

www.InspirActiveSolutions.com

Thank you for investing your valuable time to read *Think Differently, 2nd edition*!

To stay in touch and receive motivational newsletters and other free resources, please visit www.kevincsnyder.com!

Free E-books, podcasts and articles are also available on
www.kevincsnyder.com/resources

"Life has a tendency to live up the expectations we have for it!"

Expect Success – Envision it!

Made in the USA
Charleston, SC
29 May 2014